# Catherine Walker

TWENTY FIVE YEARS 1977-2002

BRITISH COUTURE

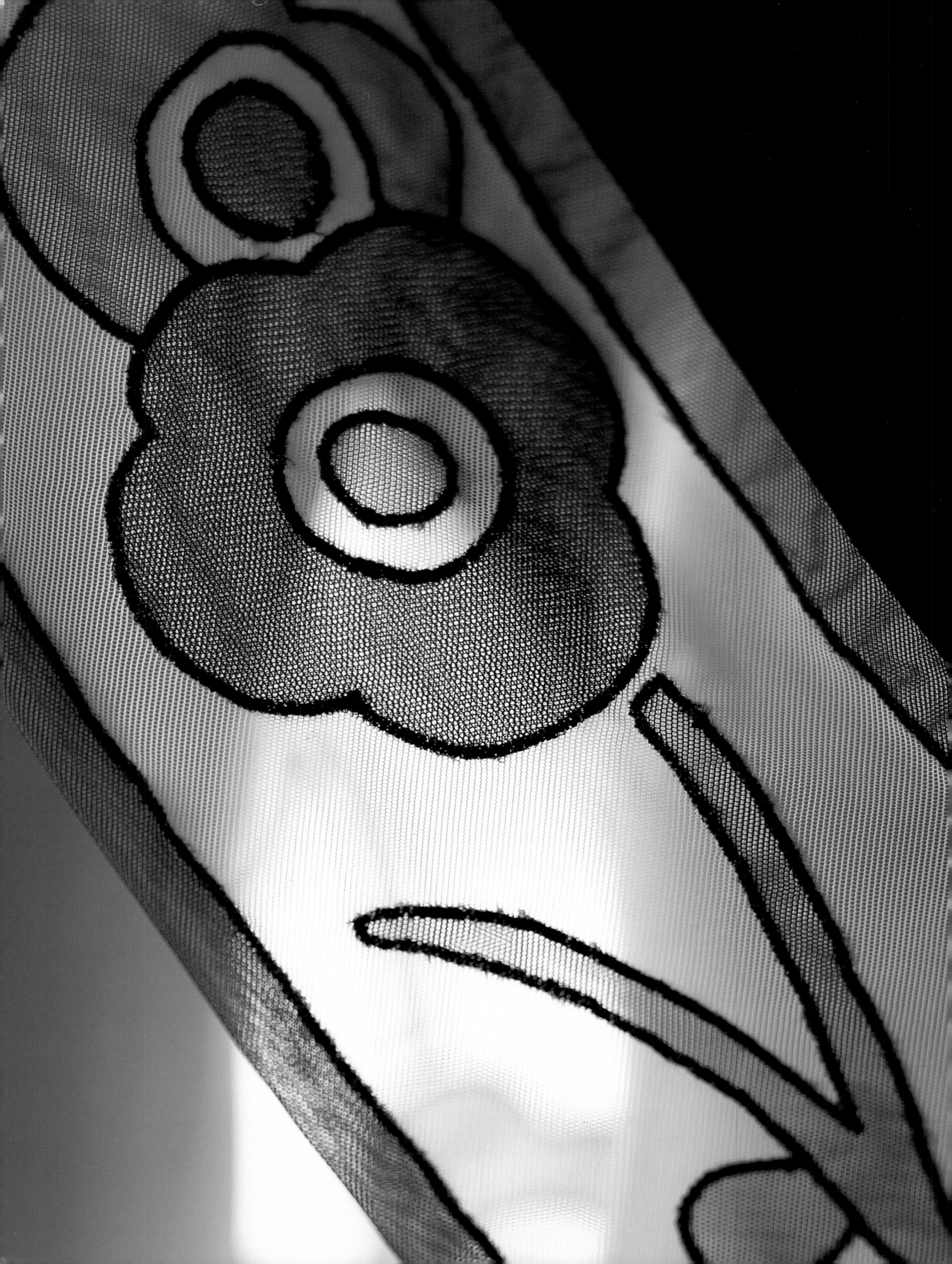

# Catherine Walker

TWENTY FIVE YEARS 1977-2002

BRITISH COUTURE

Alluring 'nude' silk dresses with revelatory lace panels, bias-cut gowns that glide around the feminine form, and corset-laced tailoring from recent collections; these often elicit the remark 'I didn't know Catherine Walker did that!'

As favourite designer of the late Diana, Princess of Wales, it is the wardrobe she created for her most famous, elegant client that sealed Catherine Walker's reputation and revealed her couture skills to a worldwide audience. Whilst the Princess' wardrobe was undoubtedly fashionable and inspired broader trends, it could be argued that it was not fashion per se. Catherine Walker's primary role for Princess Diana was to design clothes to consolidate the Princess's position as ambassador of the British royal family, whilst embracing her evolving personal taste and style. It takes a highly talented, discreet and dedicated designer to fulfil these objectives so successfully and with such aplomb. Fashion, however, is a different taskmaster. Fashion permits folly, it delights in suggestion and it celebrates ephemerality. Avoiding short-lived and outrageous gestures, Catherine Walker designs clothes that have classic overtones and are, above all, beguiling. What marks her out is her ability to create clothes that caress and move seamlessly with the wearer — ultimately, they are clothes that celebrate the feminine body. In a fashion era dominated by headline-catching, outré, 'directional' designs, it is timely to pause and contemplate the beauty and lasting appeal of Catherine Walker's collections.

To coincide with a major display of Catherine Walker's work at the Victoria & Albert Museum in 2002, this text analyses the designer's unique style as a leading and highly successful couturière, working within the British fashion industry for the past twenty-five years.

Emphasising the natural body, Catherine Walker's recent fashion designs reveal her evolving preoccupation with 'lightness of touch'. Especially innovative are clothes that highlight feminine contours and offer flirtatious glimpses of the body that is only partially concealed within. These designs have 'attitude', celebrating the modern woman's freedom to take pleasure in displaying her body, in denial of early feminist criticism that body-conscious apparel implied subjugation. Single-layer, déshabillé dresses create a frisson between body and gossamer-fine cloth, suggesting that the wearer is both dressed and undressed.

During the 1930s élite fashion explored notions of underwear as outerwear. It was seen at its best in Charles James's coquettish 'corselette' dresses, Lucien Lelong's gowns with decorative brassieres (both 1937), and Madeleine Vionnet's delicate lingerie-inspired designs. This expression can be analysed within the context of the surrealists, who delighted in challenging the status quo by reversing accepted ideas and practices surrounding interior and exterior, public and private spaces. With its intimate relationship to the body, clothing provided fertile ground for experimentation, and the underwear/outerwear dichotomy has aroused fashion sensibilities ever since. At the dawn of the twenty-first century, fetishistic trends vie with subtle, sensual interpretations; Catherine Walker's designs encapsulate the latter.

For her spring/summer 2001 collection, the designer presented lace dresses with threads intricately cut away to form opaque apertures or side panels that were virtually sheer. Composed of flesh-toned silks, Catherine Walker's dresses clothe the body whilst suggesting nudity. Outerwear and underwear become one (it is impossible to wear brassiere or pants beneath) and thus a single layer of cloth flows over the body, its perfectly smooth line undisturbed by unsightly ridges. Sensuality

is not only visual, it also involves touch: the pleasure of these dresses can be relished in equal measure by both wearer and observer.

Rebecca Arnold has written that, 'The ambiguity of underwear as outerwear, caught forever between dress and undress, has a disturbing yet fascinating erotic effect, playing on our fear of the uncertain. We are unsure how to respond to the sight of women seemingly dressed to go out and yet clad only in transparent fabrics and items of lingerie. Such styles are usually the preserve of the young, who are more willing to expose their bodies and whose bodies are inevitably more in line with fashionable ideals of youthful slenderness.' *(2)* It is often said that women designers create for their own silhouette. This is certainly true of Catherine Walker, who is slender and tall and whose body-conscious designs are shown to maximum effect upon women of similar physical type.

Much of Catherine Walker's output reveals a modern, minimal aesthetic. In order to highlight essentials, the couturière strips away the superfluous. This process of reduction and simplification focuses the eye upon that which is significant and faultlessly executed. Catherine Walker has perfected this approach. A striking black dress for autumn/winter 2001/2002, made in Clerici double silk crêpe with sheer black georgette panels adjoined by tiny black beads, emphasises and elongates the line of the body whilst also highlighting the garment construction. The opaque areas draw our attention to the fluidity between dress and body. A black V-neck sheath dress for spring/summer 2002, meticulously stitched from panels of silk satin cut on the bias, and georgette cut on the straight, provides another example of a garment designed to emphasise body and garment form. A demanding discipline, couture requires the skills of a creative designer as well as those of an exceptional technician. Seemingly effortless anthems to simplicity, Catherine Walker's designs belie highly complex pattern cutting and meticulous attention to every detail. Indeed, her immaculately executed garments can withstand the closest scrutiny and — rarely in today's fashion world — reveal the finest craft skills more commonly associated with historical haute couture.

FACING Serena Linley looks supremely elegant, dressed in Catherine Walker's scarlet corset-laced evening gown at a party thrown by Elton John.
**Photograph: oksyndication.com**

ABOVE Joely Richardson, seen here with Catherine Walker, chose the designer's gently provocative black lace and flesh-toned silk dress with sheer mesh side panels, to wear to the London Film Festival, November 2000.
**Photograph: Tim Rooke / REX Features**

# Catherine Walker

Designs by the Parisian couturière Madeleine Vionnet, acclaimed for introducing the bias cut in the 1920s and spearheading the vogue for elongated, neo-classical style evening gowns during the 1930s, have proved inspirational to Catherine Walker. Cutting on the bias (across the grain) exploits the natural elasticity of the fabric, permitting it to encircle and emphasise the feminine body. It moulds yet permits ease of movement. The juxtaposition of matt and shiny panels on a full-length evening dress for spring/summer 2001 creates a subtle interplay of light and shadow (a favourite Catherine Walker technique), and the resulting spiral effect visually elongates the body. Presented in palest cloud grey, the silk satin is used alternatively on the face and reverse of the cloth. Catherine Walker does not experiment widely with colour, generally preferring a palette of exquisitely subtle neutrals and shades of darker colour, sometimes injected with a splash of pure, brilliant red.

A philosophy graduate, Catherine Walker is a self-taught designer who started her career making children's clothes. Especially desirable were the frocks that she cut longer and narrower than those that were currently available. This elongated line has remained one of her most notable signatures. Catherine Walker's sketches depict the female body with a long, single stroke. Once fabricated, we see evening gowns with lines that flow unbroken from shoulder to hem, sometimes with trains that ripple gracefully to the floor. This lengthening effect is achieved by stretching rather than catching the waist. Because they can visually divide and foreshorten the body, waist seams at the natural level are avoided. Instead, many recent designs are high-waisted and, where necessary, nipped in at the back, rather than at the sides. It is this insistence upon an elongated line that underlies the designer's exceptional talent for creating evening gowns and cocktail dresses.

Catherine Walker embarked upon her design career as a young widow with two daughters to support. She describes how 'At first I threw myself into my work with a vigour that was fuelled by a need to control my pain and sorrow. I loved the reassuring throb of the machine and the tactile sensation of the cloth under my fingers.' *(3)* Throughout history the rhythmic and creative processes of stitching have salved the bereaved. During the eighteenth and nineteenth centuries, mourning samplers were painstakingly embroidered in black thread, whilst in more recent years quilts constructed from panels, each stitched in memory of someone who died from AIDS, have also offered solace. Catherine Walker taught herself to sew, a skill that was to equip the young mother with both a flexible means of earning a living and a constructive form of therapy.

OPPOSITE Geri Halliwell wearing a white Schlaepfer silk satin bias cut dress with silk georgette side panels at the NRJ Awards in Cannes, February 2002.
**Photograph: Big Pictures**

ABOVE For an article featuring contemporary evening gowns Tasha de Vasconcelos was photographed wearing her Catherine Walker bias-cut gown for *Vogue* August 2001.
Tasha de Vasconcelos describes the gown as *'exquisite'* and *'enchanting'*. 'I chose to wear this dress because it reminded me of the style that Catherine created for Princess Diana. What I love is the timeless elegance of Catherine's designs.'
**Photograph: Philip Berryman @ Vogue/The Condé Nast Publications**

In February 1977 Catherine Walker acquired a dilapidated town house in Sydney Street, Chelsea, which she renovated, turning the ground floor into the small shop which she retains today. (It is a remarkable coincidence that in 1881 the building had belonged to Eleanor George, a widow with two daughters and a seamstress at the court of Queen Victoria.) For some years Catherine Walker called her business The Chelsea Design Company. 'In Paris if you open a shop and put your name on the door, people will laugh at you unless you have the talent to back it up.' *(4)* It is only since 1986 that Catherine Walker has designed under her own name. During the early years she was to become consumed by the techniques of sewing and garment construction. 'I was developing an eye for fitting through my tiny clients and I was learning body proportion through doing endless minute adjustments.' *(5)* It was perhaps a natural progression that her first designs for adults were maternity dresses.

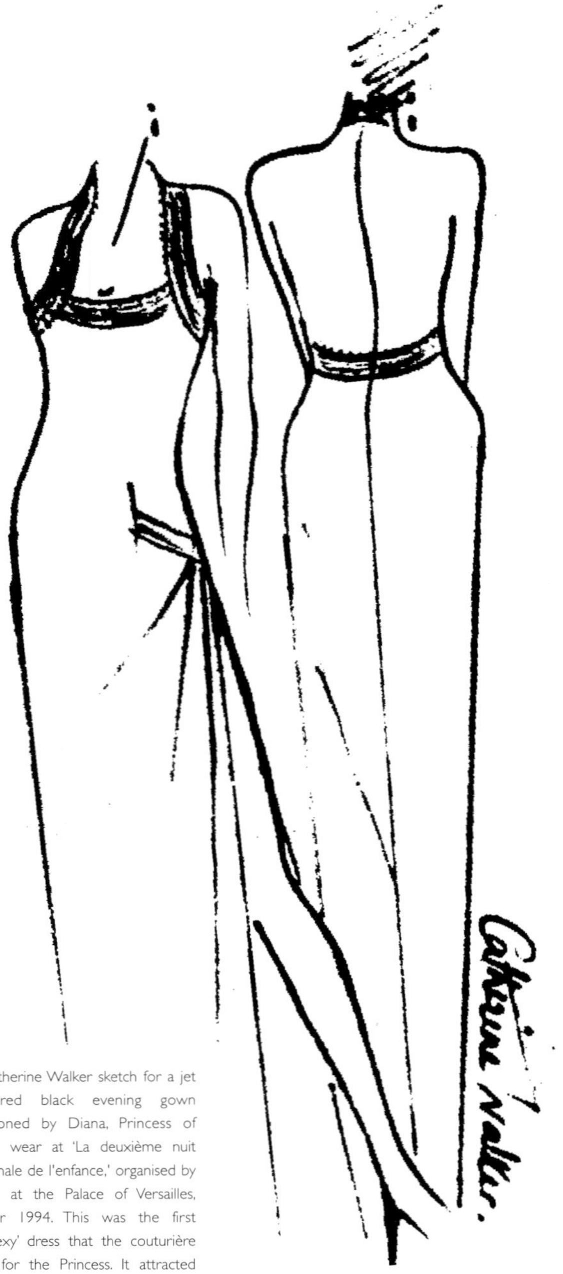

ABOVE Catherine Walker sketch for a jet embroidered black evening gown commissioned by Diana, Princess of Wales to wear at 'La deuxième nuit internationale de l'enfance,' organised by UNESCO at the Palace of Versailles, December 1994. This was the first overtly 'sexy' dress that the couturière designed for the Princess. It attracted much favourable comment: Pierre Cardin stated, '*This is the home of the Sun King of France, now we have the Sun Princess of Versailles.*'

By 1981 Catherine Walker was ready to diversify and extend her talents. Her new collection of understated cocktail and evening dresses enjoyed instant acclaim and was featured in Vogue magazine. However, before she ceased making them, it was the maternity dresses that became headline news via the patronage of the new Princess of Wales. Following the birth of her first son, the Princess invited Catherine Walker to continue designing for her public and private roles. This aspect of the designer's career has been documented extensively.*(6)* Here, it is important to emphasise that the lean silhouette she created for the Princess projected a modernity that was revolutionary for a member of the British royal family. In turn, the Princess's sartorial requirements fuelled Catherine Walker's talents, encouraging her to develop, for example, exceptional skills in embroidery and tailoring.

The couturière's first major embroidery project was a commission from the Princess for her state visit to the United Arab Emirates in March 1989. The designer chose to create an embroidery that evoked an English country garden whilst using a base colour that was fitting for the Gulf States. She chose an amethyst coloured silk and conceived a chenille and silk embroidery design with diamanté and beads depicting roses, tilted as if to catch the light as in nature. The work was executed by the London-based embroidery company S. Lock Ltd. (Established in the 1950s, Lock is the only UK firm offering a comprehensive

service to designers.) Tactile, three-dimensional embroidery has subsequently become one of Catherine Walker's hallmarks. The embroidery on this dress was so precious and remarkable that the garment was re-modelled into a straight silhouette for the Princess's state visit to Korea in November 1992. Catherine Walker insists upon designing her own embroideries and creates schemes that are mainly naturalistic - flowers, leaves and birds. The rose, interpreted in various guises from botanical perfection to abstracted art deco, is a recurring motif.

The creation of an embroidered couture gown is a highly skilled, time-consuming and costly procedure, involving five main processes. Initially a toile (the design made up in calico to check fit) is made, upon which the embroidery design is first drawn. The embroiderers then receive detailed instructions on how to interpret the design and they produce a small sample using the embroidery techniques selected by the designer. Once this is correct, a graphic is accurately made on the flat pattern of the gown and transferred onto the fabric using powdered chalk. The embroidery is then carried out, which can involve a hundred or more hours of skilled work. The dress is made for a fitting and, once any adjustments have been made, it is returned to the embroiderers to finish the design over the seams. Finally, the completed dress is ready to be presented to the client. In 1986 Catherine Walker opened a second shop, on London's Fulham Road, a glass conservatory specialising in couture bridal wear. Some of the designer's most outstanding embroideries have been undertaken for this section of the business.

LEFT Lady Gabriella Windsor wearing an apricot Buche silk gown embroidered with silk roses from the 'English rose' collection spring/summer 2001, to attend the post-christening party of the Greek royal family's grandson at Syon House.
**Photograph: Nunn Syndication**

For Lady Helen Windsor's wedding gown Catherine Walker spent many hours in St George's Chapel studying the windows, the shapes of which, together with the motifs of the Kent tiara, were worked into the embroidery. Describing the brides choice of dress, Vogue reported, 'The effect will be not so much fairytale as beautiful and inspiring - not the happy ending to a golden romance but the beginning of a real love story.' *(7)*

An altogether different bridal ensemble was created for Jemima Goldsmith's wedding to Imran Khan in June 1995. Based on the traditional dress of Pakistan, Catherine Walker created a shalwar kameez in aquamarine Taroni georgette with an embroidered design inspired by a tiara, presenting a fusion of European and Pakistani influences. This style, also worn by Diana, Princess of Wales was subsequently to exert a major influence on international fashion.

The bridal gown for Catrina Skepper's marriage to Count Alessandro dei Conti Guerrini Maraldi in May 2000 represents one of Catherine Walker's major creative accomplishments and is a testimony to the skills and workmanship within her couture house. Already a loyal client, Catrina Skepper gave the designer a free rein allowing her imagination to fully take hold. Her initial inspiration came from a fragment of Goutarel lace. Because of the client's height and personality, a design with a generous motif was possible. After the initial toile was approved, another preparatory model, this time in the precious lace, was made to see how the pattern would work. The completed wedding gown features an epaules denudees neckline, fitted bodice, sheer fluted sleeves and a low-cut back that gently cascades into a flowing skirt, concealing ten layers of fluffy organza. The lace is illuminated with a staggering 44,000 pearl and crystal beads and meticulously re-embroidered by hand with 300 metres of duchess satin cording to echo the elongated silhouette. Most of this work was conducted in-house. Catrina Skepper recalls her delight at the finished work, describing it as a magical, fairytale gown that, whilst being extensively worked, was visually simple, fluid and surprisingly comfortable. Re-iterating her faith in the designer, she states 'I knew however far Catherine went she would never lose sight of the fact that it was me — Catrina — wearing the dress.' *(8)*

LEFT Jemima Goldsmith and Imran Khan on their wedding day, 21 June 1995. Embroidered aqua Taroni georgette shalwar kameez.
**Photograph: REX Features**

OPPOSITE Lady Helen Windsor and Mr Timothy Taylor, 18 July1992.
The bride's dress, made in silk zibeline, featured a pearl and diamond embroidered curled neckline and cathedral length train. It was cut in ten full-length flared panels to emphasise the fluidity of the body.
**Photograph: Chrisopher Simon-Sykes / Camera Press**

OVERLEAF Catrina Skepper wearing her magnificent wedding gown
**Photograph: John Swannell**

Catherine Walker's first tailored design was a dashing red barathea wool double-breasted coat with black velvet trim designed for Diana, Princess of Wales in 1984. That year the desiger had attended an exhibition of works by fashion photographer John French at the Victoria & Albert Museum curated by Valerie Mendes. Based in London, French's black and white photographs captured perfectly the glamour and aristocratic hauteur of top models such as Barbara Goalen, immaculately attired in early post-war fashions, often tailored by English designers. Catherine Walker marvelled at the styles and photographic techniques that, some thirty years on, struck a contemporary note, capturing modern femininity and elongating the body.

From the 1870s through to the 1950s London was revered for its male designer tailors - from Redfern to Digby Morton - who created superb ensembles for women. However, by the mid-1980s this tradition had all but vanished, and Catherine Walker's man-tailored designs were to strike a new fashion note. After much searching, she was introduced to a tailor called George Tebboth, who became a highly valued member of staff who still works exclusively with the company today. Mr Tebboth has an exceptional precision and a lightness of touch capable of evoking the elegance of John French's images. Working together, they elongated the torso through the structured approach of tailoring. Since this time, Catherine Walker has eliminated unnecessary details throughout her collection and focused upon streamlined garments that permit the full sweep of the silhouette.

Especially noteworthy amongst her tailored designs include the military-red broad-shouldered wool coat punctuated with a plastron of gold buttons and modelled by Naomi Campbell in Vogue November 1987. Rendered more fluid, the same design executed in red velvet was selected for the September issue of Harpers & Queen. Open jackets without fastenings and collarless jackets were amongst Catherine Walker's influential signature designs of the 1980s and 1990s. By removing weight and superfluous detail, these jackets served to visually lengthen the neck and, in turn, to emphasise the face. Above all, Catherine Walker seeks to create fashions that subtly draw attention to the beauty of her client, rather than bold design statements that can overshadow the wearer.

ABOVE Olivia Williams was photographed for the cover of the Sunday Telegraph Magazine wearing this black, fine-ribbed wool, short jacket with metal eyelets and silk satin laced corset detail, (autumn/winter 2001-2002).
**Photograph: Robert Wyatt**

FACING Naomi Campbell models a red wool, military style jacket for Vogue November 1987. The proportion of the eighties shoulder-line over the high-waisted jersey leggings emphasizes the elongation of the torso. The graduated military buttons punctuate the extension of the body.
**Photograph: Hans Feurer / The Condé Nast Publications Ltd**

Variations on masculine 'le smoking' tailored jackets become overtly feminine in Catherine Walker's hands and, in black wool with satin detailing, form a mainstay of her collections. Eschewing the emphatically masculine cut of these garments she has introduced a lean, contemporary 'le smoking' which features a pronounced cleavage, soft shoulder line and light construction. The design has also been adapted to form a bustier jacket and a perfectly smart, double-breasted evening dress. Reflecting current preoccupations with the body-garment symbiosis, a fluid tailored suit in black crêpe for autumn/winter 2001—2002 has split seams, evocative of sixteenth century slashed work. The designer challenges our expectations of élite couture by offering a suit quite literally coming apart at the seams. This ploy creates a decorative effect and again emphasises construction. For spring/summer 2002 her collection is inspired by the pert and feminine styles worn by Jackie Onassis and includes a prim, high-waisted tuxedo coat dress in black wool and silk, modernised by the use of open, beaded seams.

'The French are sexy, the English sensual — I try and merge the two' (9) states Catherine Walker. Although she was born in France, she considers herself a quintessentially English designer and emphasises that if she tried to work in Paris her designs would lose their 'hazy' quality. Though the English culture is inspirational, working as a couturier in London is extraordinarily challenging. Fashion is a notoriously volatile business and this is especially true in Britain.

Unlike their French, Italian and American colleagues, high fashion designers in London are barely supported by state or industry, neither do they enjoy extensive patronage from wealthy clients. (Although British women spend only marginally less than other Europeans or Americans on clothing, they generally buy more and cheaper — a fact often interpreted as a tribute to our high street stores.) This can partly be explained by the powerful Protestant ethic that holds in contempt the ephemeral and narcissistic qualities associated with fashion - since it is constantly changing it can be of no lasting value. Although the British have special affection for highly creative 'amateurism', in the case of fashion it rarely stretches to developing and financing ideas and

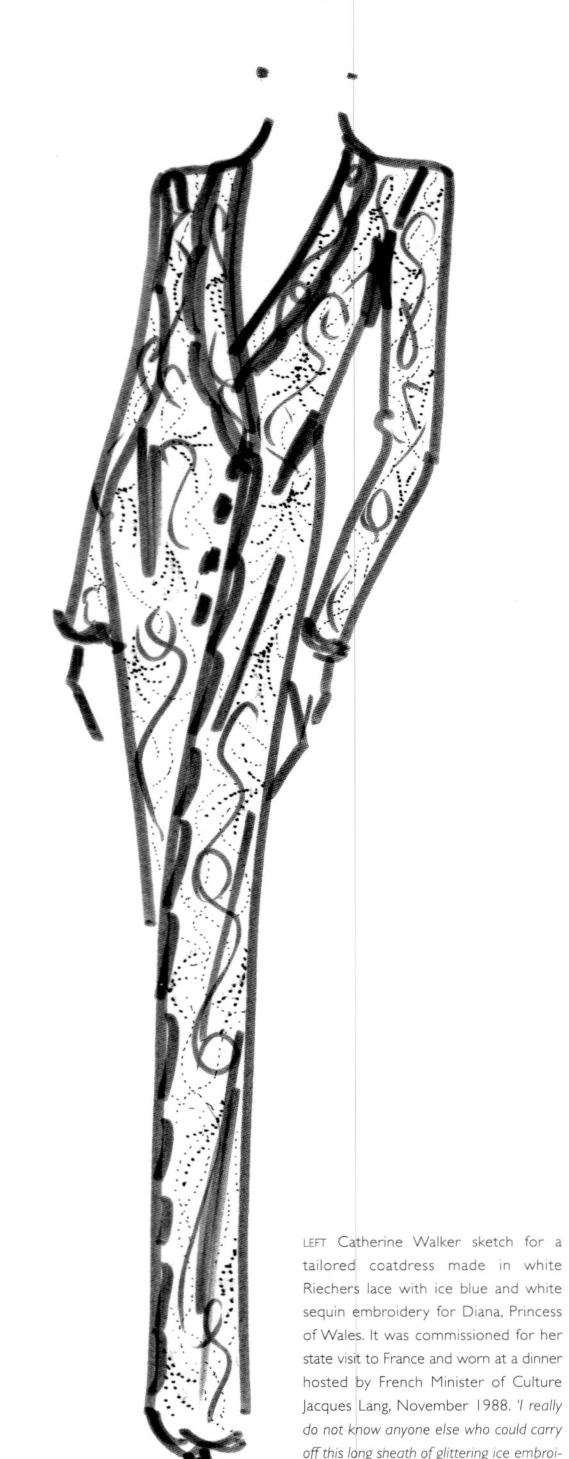

LEFT Catherine Walker sketch for a tailored coatdress made in white Riechers lace with ice blue and white sequin embroidery for Diana, Princess of Wales. It was commissioned for her state visit to France and worn at a dinner hosted by French Minister of Culture Jacques Lang, November 1988. *'I really do not know anyone else who could carry off this long sheath of glittering ice embroidery in quite the way The Princess of Wales did.'* Catherine Walker.

turning them into viable business. In spite of full order-books, all too often British designers have gone out of business because they could not raise the capital investment required. Catherine Walker has been fortunate that her second husband is an astute businessman and manages these affairs, permitting her to focus upon the creative and technical aspects of design. The combination of these dual talents has given rise to an English couture house that enjoys impressive commercial success.

Haute couture in London has always operated on a relatively small scale. Conversely, designers working in Paris, Milan and New York often secure major capital investment to develop highly lucrative licensing and retail opportunities. The sales of these licensed goods and diffusion lines provide their revenue, while catwalk shows serve to showcase the brand image. To ensure maximum publicity such designers present fashion extremes in an exciting and theatrical medium. In Britain, with few exceptions, the sole product that the relatively small-scale and mostly designer-owned couture houses have to sell is the clothes. These factors in part explain why British couture has always enjoyed a reputation for wearability, and Catherine Walker fits within this continuum.

Until the seventeenth century the making of luxurious clothing was a profession undertaken by male tailors, but in 1675 a law was passed in Paris that was to change this. On completing a three-year apprenticeship in cutting and dressmaking, women were permitted to work as couturières, or seamstresses. Dressmaking soon became an industry dominated by women, the most famous being Mlle Rose Bertin, dressmaker to Queen Marie Antoinette. However, Bertin was not considered a true creator; her designs were largely dictated by the desires of her clients. It was the young Englishman, Charles Frederick Worth, who is widely credited for being the first couturier and admired as an arbiter of fashionable taste. Patronised by the Empress Eugénie, Worth was to become world famous, and his premises in the rue de la Paix, the creative core of the modern fashion industry.

ABOVE Diana, Princess of Wales wears a black barathea tailored tuxedo jacket with white ottoman collar, lapels and cuffs and a waistcoat with jet buttons from the autumn/winter 1992-93 collection. Although the suit was originally designed with trousers, the Princess asked for a short skirt for her first public engagement after the announcement of her separation. This body skimming, structured design with trompe l'oeil effect exemplifies the designer's tailoring at this time.
**Photograph: Tim Graham**

Emerging in the era of the sewing machine, and the consequent de-skilling and greater democratisation of the fashion system, haute couture has always championed artistry and the work of the artisan. Like fine art, true couture is unashamedly élite, patronised today by just some two to three thousand women worldwide, although relished by a great many more.

Implicit in the term 'haute couture' is a supreme quality of creative and innovative design and workmanship, with the provision of an individual made-to-measure service. (Translated literally 'couture' means 'sewing' or 'needlework'.) Alas, the terms are all too often misused in Britain, applied generically to describe custom-made clothing irrespective of standard. However, in Paris, the prestigious trade organisation the Chambre Syndicale (established in 1868) issues strict criteria for designers seeking to use this legally protected term.

To qualify as an haute couturier in Paris a company must design fashions that are made to order with one or more fittings for a specific client. It must employ at least twenty people in its workshop and present a collection of at least fifty designs, day and evening garments for spring/summer and autumn/winter, to the press. Catherine Walker doesn't stage a fashion show because there would be no financial advantage in doing so, although she rues the absence of a public platform to show her designs. Otherwise, her business fulfils these criteria.

Catherine Walker's atelier is run along Parisian lines, with separate studios devoted to tailoring (coats and suits made of flat pieces cut from patterns) and flou (dressmaking, involving drapery using more pliant cloths), with additional skilled craftspeople employed to undertake embroidery. Within haute couture the repetition of a model for an individual client is often entrusted to one person, whereas at ready-to-wear level, workers generally specialise in one part of the making process and a garment is passed through several hands. The vendeuses (talented salespersons) possess intimate knowledge of each client's taste

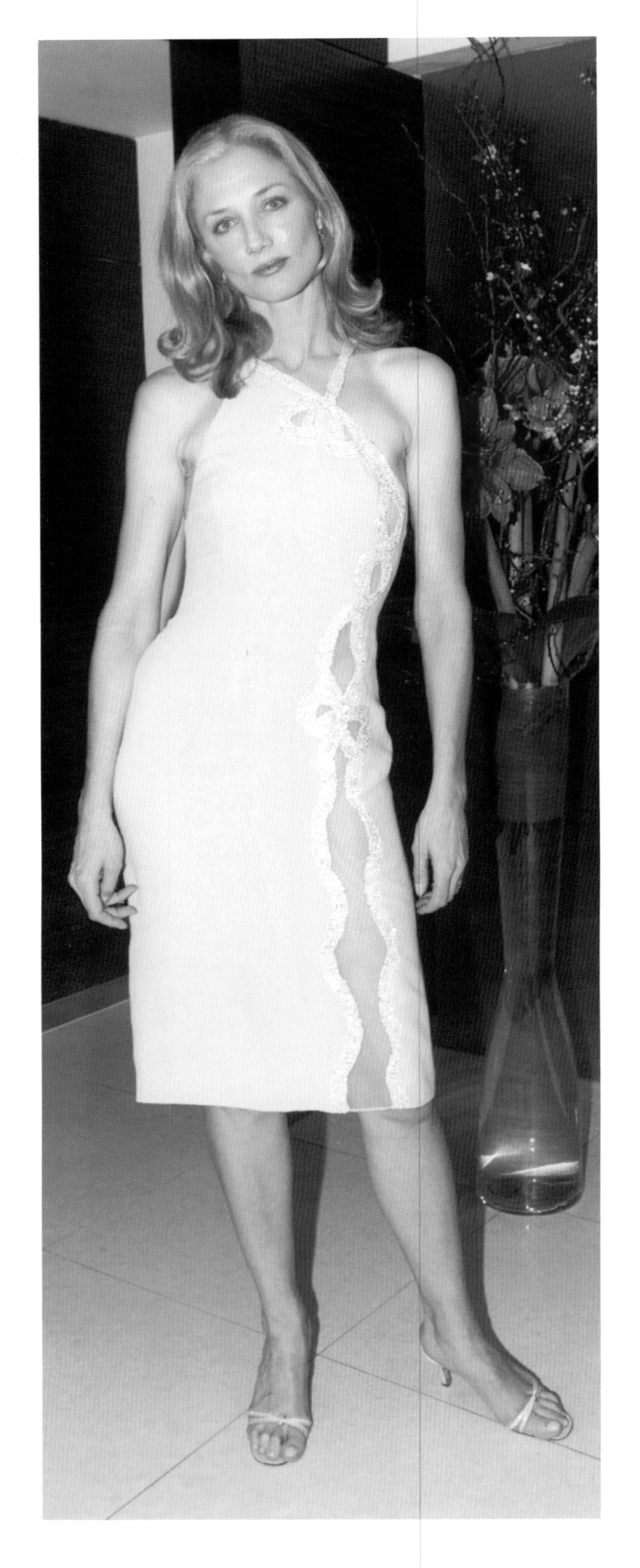

and figure type. They are responsible for taking fittings and communicating the information about each client to the relevant studio.

In London there have been various short-lived organisations, such as the 'British Couture Collections' formed in 1989, but today no such body exists to represent and consolidate the specific interests of London's couturiers. (As early as 1900 French houses showed their collections together to promote their product at home and overseas.) Following the closure of Norman Hartnell and Victor Edelstein in 1993, the British Fashion Council withdrew its category for Couture at the British Fashion Awards. This had formed the major, publicity-laden, annual trade event to celebrate this area of British achievement (Catherine Walker won the prestigious award for British Couture in 1990 and the British Glamour award in 1991). Today there remains a very small coterie of London couturiers.

LEFT To attend Princess Margaret's seventieth birthday party, Viscountess Serena Linley wore Catherine Walker's lace and organza evening dress from the 'Time regained' collection for autumn/winter 1999-2000

**Photograph: Nunn Syndication**

OPPOSITE Joely Richardson at the opening party of *Lady Windermere's Fan*, March 2002.

**Photograph: Alan Davidson for peoplenews.com**

# Catherine Walker

The most exclusive fashion journals continue to present the work of the London couture, but elite fashion has found a new showcase within the plethora of lifestyle magazines, notably OK! and Hello in Britain. With their extensive features and numerous photographic spreads designed to fuel our celebrity-driven culture, the clothing worn by the rich and famous is spotlighted. Top-league actresses have become modern-day supermodels, their appearance as front-row guests at fashion shows often of greater public interest than either the collection being shown or its creator. Thus their choice of clothes and favourite designers are carefully scrutinised by the media, and the financial ramifications for the houses that dress them are all too obvious.

Catherine Walker's meticulously kept archive houses a mountain of press books dating back to the 1970s. As she is publicity shy, the company chooses to avoid a proactive press strategy. Not surprisingly, therefore, information about Catherine Walker herself and her working practices is scant. Instead, press coverage converges upon her designs and lifestyles of her high-profile clientele. A notable exceptional, was an article in the Mail on Sunday in 1998, in which Diana, Princess of Wales was photographed with Catherine Walker and her team of skilled craftspeople at Kensington Palace, just prior to the charity auction of the Princess's clothes at Christies. In this sale, fifty of the eighty ensembles were designed by Catherine Walker.

Over the years, Catherine Walker has been a regular visitor to the archives of the Victoria & Albert Museum's magnificent Textiles and Dress Collection. She has examined the cut of an early twentieth century tailored jacket by the English designer Redfern, seen fragile 1930s couture-made lingerie and marvelled at Vionnet's understated day dresses and technically complex evening gowns. In turn, she has offered to donate her own designs. A T-bar choker evening dress in black Buche silk velvet, inspired by Cartier's `Garland Style' jewels, for spring/summer 1997, was selected for display the same year in the V&A's exhibition 'The Cutting Edge; 50 Years of British Fashion', curated by the author. The soot-black velvet proved the perfect base for the icy clear diamanté and silver filigree work that formed a vertical back pendant emphasising the sensuality of the spine.

It is appropriate that in 2002 the V&A should invite Catherine Walker to stage a display of some fifty garments drawn from her own archive within the Dress Collection, the gallery that celebrates some four centuries of fashionable dress. Some of the exhibits selected for this twenty-fifth anniversary are shown in the full-length photographs and captivating details within this book.

ABOVE Diana, Princess of Wales with Catherine Walker and the couture team who had supplied the Princess with a seamless flow of couture garments for sixteen years. The Princess was to auction many of these creations and asked for the 'team' to be photographed with her as a prelude to the sale.

**Photograph: Tim Graham**

OPPOSITE A rare photograph of Catherine Walker with Diana, Princess of Wales, who commissioned this pale blue Taroni silk crêpe shift dress (spring/summer 1997) with 'ice rose' embroidery, for Christie's gala evening to support the auction of her dresses in 1997. *'Here the bugle beads and diamanté are so dense that they rise from the surface of the fabric like florets made of sugar.'* Catherine Walker.

**Photograph: Tim Graham**

# Catherine Walker

In examining Catherine Walker's work one becomes aware of a visual poetry and tenderness that permeates her designs - she describes them as 'emotional, clothes to fall in love in'. Catherine Walker is all too aware of human frailty, not only that of others but also her own. In 1995 she was diagnosed with breast cancer, a serious illness that resulted in her loving and appreciating women's bodies all the more. Indeed, the very temporality of feminine beauty has fuelled her desire to capture it. Hovering between the past and future, yet resolutely of the present, fashion is her vehicle.

Catherine Walker
AUTUMN/WINTER
1999-2000 collection

*'Time regained'*

**Flesh toned Clerici silk crêpe dress with black glass beads**

Reflecting on the belle époque, Catherine Walker interpreted references from late 19th - early 20th century design with a 21st century modernity. The curvilinear shape of the Art Nouveau floral design follows and accentuates the line of the body on this three-quarter-length evening gown with scoop neckline.

OPPOSITE Detail. Thousands of tiny, glossy caviare-like glass beads were hand-sewn to create this unusual stencil reverse graphic design.

Catherine Walker
AUTUMN/WINTER
2001-2002 collection

*'Le sens de la peau'*
*(The Awareness of the Flesh)*

**Cocktail dress in black Solstiss lace on flesh silk georgette and flesh toned mesh**

Exploring ideas surrounding dress and undress, Catherine Walker's halter-neck gown, with its graduating sheer apertures, provides veiled glimpses of the feminine body. The geometric lines of the dress are softened by the leg-revealing asymmetric hemline, which is intricately hand-worked around the lace design.

Catherine Walker
AUTUMN/WINTER
2001/2002 collection

*'Le sens de la peau'*
*(The Awareness of the Flesh)*

**Black cocktail dress in Taroni georgette on flesh georgette, with black duchesse silk satin-panelled ribbons punched with metal eyelets**

The eyelets have been taken from corsetry, but instead of being used functionally, they are inserted to reveal peep holes along the body, running through the bust and hip line.

Catherine Walker
AUTUMN/WINTER
2001-2002 collection

*'Le sens de la peau'*
*(The Awareness of the Flesh)*

**Black Clerici silk double crepe dress with thread and diamante-embroidered mesh**

A little black cocktail dress is given a seductive twist with its sheer shoulder to hem side panels. The lattice effect of the embroidery was inspired by the technical construction and weave of hosiery.

Catherine Walker
AUTUMN/WINTER
2001-2002 collection

*'Le sens de la peau'*
*(The Awareness of the Flesh)*

**Black Schlaepfer sargent silk dress with embroidered eyelets**

The stark, almost Puritan, cut of this dress is lightened by the contrasting and unconventional fastening. The threading of over 300 eyelets follows the shape of the body, acting as superficial seams. Each section relies upon the thread-work to hold the dress together.

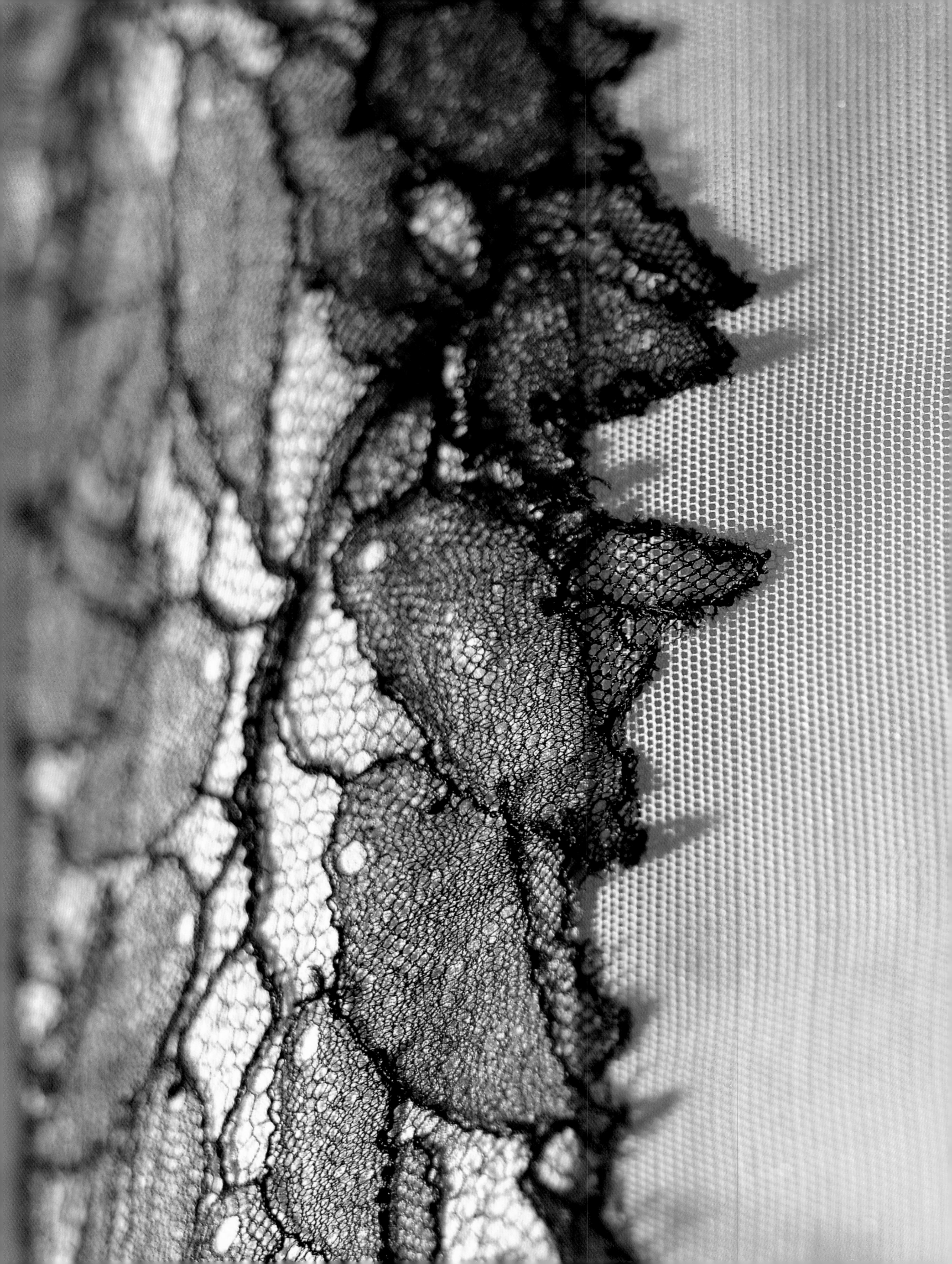

Catherine Walker
AUTUMN/WINTER
1999-2000 collection

*'Time regained'*

**Black Solstiss foliate lace dress on flesh coloured silk georgette, with sheer mesh side panels**

This lingerie-inspired dress reflects perfectly Catherine Walker's interest in lighter, sexier designs. The black lace panel, intricately hand-cut around the leaf design, serves to narrow and elongate the body, whilst the sheer flesh-toned silk precludes the wearing of underwear and suggests nudity.

OPPOSITE Detail.

Catherine Walker
SPRING/SUMMER
2001 collection

*'English rose'*

**Platinum Tessutti silk satin dress**

Emphasising the circular bias cut of the dress and exploiting the reverse and face sides of the cloth, Catherine Walker has created a subtle decorative chevron effect that visually elongates the body. The asymmetric line is continued through to the one shoulder neckline.

Catherine Walker
SPRING/SUMMER
2001 collection

*'English rose'*

**Apricot Buche silk georgette dress with silk embroidery and sheer mesh back panels**

Oversize roses hand-embroidered in self-colour silk thread, meander around the gown to create a subtle hazy effect that characterises much of Catherine Walker's work. The narrow back panel emphasises the sensuality of the spine, whilst the sheer side sections of this circular trained evening gown reveal the body within.

Catherine Walker
SPRING/SUMMER
1998 collection

**White Clerici silk georgette dress with chenille embroidery**

Ethereal, yet rendered relatively informal by its cap sleeves, this cruise dress features a rounded neckline and circular train. The light, sheer quality of the georgette perfectly offsets the flight of swallows that encircles the body.

Catherine Walker
SPRING/SUMMER
1998 collection

**Apricot Buche silk georgette embroidered dress with beads and sequins**

A delicate floral embroidery embellishes this three-quarter-length evening dress. The asymmetry of the single shoulder strap is echoed in the side split that curves to form a small train.

*'There is to the French mind a unique English aristocratic charm that translates itself into fashion in the palest colour hues and an absence of fussiness. It is something to do with textures and subtle nuances, rather than the richer, bolder play of continental shapes and colours - a discreet sensuality, rather than an up-front sexuality.'*
Catherine Walker

Catherine Walker
SPRING/SUMMER
2002 collection

**Black Schlaepfer silk satin dress with black and ivory mesh inserts**

The slender mesh inserts fall down the body to accentuate both length and slenderness, echoing some of the qualities of Erwin Blumenfeld's photographic work which has been a source of inspiration for the designer's spring/summer 2002 collection.

Catherine Walker
AUTUMN/WINTER
2001-2002 collection

*'Le sens de la peau' (The Awareness of the Flesh)*

**Black Taroni silk, flesh-tone mesh dress and Swarovski black diamanté**

Previously, Catherine Walker has used Cartier's jewellery in a more formal manner, but here, she has designed cut-away sections to create a modern twist. A Cartier garland bow is re-worked to follow the curve of the body and show a glimpse of flesh.

Catherine Walker
AUTUMN/WINTER
2001-2002 collection

*'Le sens de la peau' (The Awareness of the Flesh)*

**Black Clerici double silk crêpe dress with sheer black silk georgette and black beads**

The contrasting, solid and sheer silk panels, emphasise and elongate the lines of the body. This is reiterated by the black beads, which also serve to highlight the garment's construction.

Catherine Walker
SPRING/SUMMER
2002 collection

**Black Schlaepfer sargent silk with ivory mesh inserts**

The inspiration for this evening dress was drapery. The slender mesh inserts cut across the body, to mimic where the light would catch it if draping occurred.

Catherine Walker
AUTUMN/WINTER
1997-1998 collection

**Red Clerici silk satin dress with appliquéd roses and corded decoration**

Drawing on the romanticism of Russian folklore, the designer's inspiration was an ornate embroidered shawl that draped around the shoulders to create an impression of roses spiralling around the body. A similar effect has been created on this striking bustier gown - in bold `Valentine red rose' silk - which culminates in an asymmetric, rose-entwined shoulder strap.

OPPOSITE Detail. Each rose was hand-made and embroidered onto the dress in matching tone-on-tone silk threads.

Catherine Walker
AUTUMN/WINTER
2001-2002 collection

*'Le sens de la peau' (The Awareness of the Flesh)*

**Black Schlaepfer organza dress with sequins and black mesh**

This dress is cut on a bias that encircles the body and in contrast the stark design lines are on the straight grain.

Catherine Walker
AUTUMN/WINTER
2001-2002 collection

*'Le sens de la peau'*
*(The Awareness of the Flesh)*

**Black Schlaepfer sargeant silk satin dress with black mesh**

The bias cut of this dress emphasises the silhouette and works against the straight cut of the side panels. It was shown as part of Catherine Walkers 'Fashion in Motion' performance at the V&A in 2001 and was subsequently donated to the museum's Textiles and Dress Collection.